Wealth Code for Online Business

How to Generate Wealth Doing Online Business

DANNIS B. MOORE

Book Review

"Wealth Code for Online Business" is a comprehensive and informative book that provides practical tips and strategies for entrepreneurs looking to build successful online businesses.

Written by an experienced online business consultant, the book is designed to help individuals who are new to online business, as well as those who are already running an online business but are struggling to achieve success.

The book is divided into several chapters, each of which covers a specific aspect of online business. The first chapter provides an overview of the online business landscape and the opportunities available for entrepreneurs. The author explains the importance of identifying a niche market and developing a business plan that aligns with the market needs.

The subsequent chapters cover various topics such as creating a brand identity, developing a marketing strategy, building an online presence, and implementing effective customer service.

The author provides practical advice on how to create a unique brand identity that stands out from competitors, how to leverage social media to build a following, and how to optimise your website for search engines.
One of the key strengths of this book is that it provides actionable advice that readers can implement immediately.

The author provides real-world examples and case studies, which help readers understand how they can apply the strategies discussed in the book in their own business. Moreover, the author stresses the importance of regular evaluation and adaptation to changing market trends, which is essential for long-term success in online business.

The book is well-written, easy to read, and provides valuable insights and practical advice that can help entrepreneurs achieve their goals. I would highly recommend this book to anyone who is serious about building a successful online business.

About The Author

The author of Wealth Code for Online Business, Dannis B. Moore, is hailed as a major figure in the human potential movement. In this book, which has informative base knowledge providing practical tips and strategies for entrepreneurs looking to build successful online businesses.

He explains how you can properly achieve wealth by practically observing rules guiding wealth without being affected and traumatic.

Table of Contents

Introduction

In today's world, Online businesses have become a massive source of income for individuals and companies. With the internet reaching every corner of the globe, online businesses have the capability to reach millions of potential customers, which ultimately leads to more revenue.

However, running a successful online business requires more than just a website and a product to sell. Entrepreneurs must understand the intricacies of wealth management and how to maximise profits for their online businesses.

This Wealth Code for Online Business aims to provide valuable insights into the world of online business and how to manage and grow your wealth to achieve long-term success.

Chapter 1

DEFINITION OF ONLINE BUSINESS

Online business refers to any kind of business activity that is conducted over the internet. Such businesses can include e-commerce stores, digital product sales, online consulting services, and several others.

These businesses usually depend on online transactions and communication with customers, suppliers, and partners through websites, social media pages, or other digital platforms.

They offer the advantage of a wider geographical reach, low operating costs, and easy scalability, making them an attractive option for entrepreneurs and businesses of all sizes. Online businesses have changed the way traditional commerce is conducted and are now a significant contributor to the global economy.

Importance of Generating Wealth in Online Business

Online business has become increasingly popular in the last decade, and more people are turning to the internet to generate wealth.

The importance of generating wealth in online business cannot be overstated, as it offers numerous benefits to those who are successful. In this article, we'll explore the main reasons why generating wealth in online business is crucial.

Financial Freedom: One of the most significant benefits of generating wealth in online business is financial freedom. With a successful online business, you can create a steady stream of income that can help you achieve your financial goals and provide the freedom to live the lifestyle you desire.

Online businesses also offer a scalable income model, allowing you to continuously grow your business and increase your income.

Flexibility: Another benefit of generating wealth through online business is the flexibility it provides. With an online business, you are not limited to a specific location, and you can work from anywhere in the world.

This flexibility allows you to balance your work and personal life, and you can work at your own pace, depending on your schedule.

Low Start-up Costs: Starting an online business requires lower capital investment compared to traditional businesses. With a laptop, internet connection, and minimal software or tools, you can start an online business. This makes it more accessible for people to start and grow their own businesses, even with limited financial resources.

Equal Opportunities: Online businesses offer equal opportunities for entrepreneurs from different backgrounds. You don't need to have a huge network or connections to start a successful online business. You can leverage social media and other digital marketing tools to reach your ideal audience and grow your brand.

Diversification: Generating wealth through online business provides a way to diversify your income streams. Having multiple sources of income reduces the risk of relying on one source of income and ensures financial stability in the long run.

Automation: Many online businesses can be automated, which means that you can generate income even when you're not physically working. For example, creating digital products like ebooks or courses can provide passive income as people purchase them without you lifting a finger.

Generating wealth through online business is crucial for achieving financial freedom, flexibility, and personal growth. With the low start-up costs, equal opportunities, automation, and diversification opportunities, online business provides a unique and profitable path to success.

Chapter 2

IDENTIFY A NICHE

Identifying a niche is a crucial step in creating success through business, especially in e-commerce, and content creation. Finding a niche can help you target a specific audience and stand out among your competitors. Here are some tips on how to identify a niche.

Identify Your Interests

To narrow down your search, think about the topics you enjoy the most. Think about areas that interest you, and areas where there aren't many products, services, or content about. Oftentimes, this will shed some light on un-leveraged opportunities.

Research the Market

Do your homework on the market you intend to target. Analyse competitors, their products, and services to see how competitive the market is. If competition is stiff, it may be a good idea to explore a niche that isn't as saturated.

Identify Problems
People are always looking to solve problems. Solve a problem, and you're in business. Identify problems that currently don't have a lot of solutions, and you'll find yourself in a unique position.

Identify Gaps
There are an infinite number of possibilities and "micro-niches" within industries. Identify gaps that aren't addressed in your industry, and capitalise on those gaps.

Work with Your Skills
Your skills may help you identify potential niches that require specific skills sets. For example, if you're a great writer, starting an article writing company could be the perfect niche.

Choose a Unique Angle
When identifying your niche, choose an angle that is unique to your business in order to stand out from the competitors. Ideally, this angle

should align with your USP (Unique Selling Point).

Target a Specific Audience

Targeting a specific audience is key when identifying a niche. This way, you'll be able to create content or products that meet their unique needs.

Identifying a niche is crucial to creating a successful business. Before launching, make sure you've done your research on the market, pinpointed gaps, chosen a unique angle, and targeted a specific audience.

With the right planning, execution, and dedication, finding your niche can be the first step on the journey to prosperity.

Defining a Niche Market

Defining a niche market is an important aspect of any business strategy. A niche market is a subset of a larger market that focuses on a specific product, service, or demographic. The goal of targeting a niche market is to find a profitable and untapped market segment that can be served with a particular product, service, or solution.

The key to defining a niche market is understanding the unique needs and preferences of the target customers. This requires extensive research and analysis of the market, including consumer behaviour, attitudes, and demographics.

It is important to identify the key characteristics of the target market, including age, income, education, location, lifestyle, and buying habits. Once a niche market has been identified, it is important to develop a marketing strategy that speaks directly to the target customers.

This may involve developing a unique value proposition, creating a distinct brand identity, and tailoring messaging and marketing materials to the specific needs and preferences of the target audience.

In order to effectively target a niche market, it may be necessary to tailor products or services to the specific needs of that market. This may involve developing new products, customising existing products, or offering specialised services or solutions that meet the unique needs of the target customer.

Success in a niche market often requires a strong commitment to customer service and engagement.

This may involve developing a close relationship with target customers, providing personalised service, and offering ongoing support and resources to help customers achieve their goals.

Overall, defining a niche market requires a deep understanding of the target audience, their unique needs and preferences, and an ability to tailor products, services, and solutions to meet those needs.

By effectively targeting and serving a niche market, businesses can create a strong competitive advantage and sustainable growth over the long term.

Researching Potential Niches

Researching potential niches is an important first step in starting a new business or expanding an existing one. A niche is a specialised segment of a market that is not being adequately served by existing providers. Finding a profitable niche can be challenging, but with careful research and analysis, you can identify untapped opportunities and create a successful business.

Identify your Interests and Passions: Start by listing out your interests and passions. This will help you to identify niches that you find compelling and enjoyable to work in.

Research Market Trends: Look at current market trends and identify areas where demand is growing or where there is an emerging need. This can help you to identify potential niches that are underserved or have untapped potential.

Analyse Competition: Study your competition and identify areas where they are weak or not meeting the needs of customers. This can help you to identify potential niches that you can fill with your unique offering.

Conduct Customer Research: Talk to potential customers to understand their needs, pain points, and preferences. This can help you to identify potential niches that are not being served by existing providers.

Evaluate Profitability: Once you have identified potential niches, evaluate their profitability. Look at the cost of delivering your product or service, the price you can charge, and the potential market size. This can help you to identify niches that are financially viable.

Test The Market: Before committing significant resources to a new niche, test the market with a small-scale pilot project. This can help you to validate your assumptions, refine your offering, and identify potential challenges before investing heavily.

Monitor Trends: Keep an eye on market trends and adjust your strategy as needed. This can help you to stay ahead of the competition and remain relevant in a changing market.

Researching potential niches requires careful planning, analysis, and testing.

By following these steps, you can identify untapped opportunities, create a unique offering, and build a successful business.

Evaluating the Market Demand and Competition

Evaluating market demand and competition is a critical step in understanding the potential for success in a new business venture or expanding an existing one. A thorough evaluation can help you determine if there is sufficient demand for your product or service and if there is an opportunity to compete in the market.

Define your Target Market: Identify who your ideal customer is and what their needs and pain points are. This will help you to determine the size of your potential market and identify any gaps in the market that you could fill.

Research your Target Market: Conduct research to understand your target market's preferences, habits, and buying patterns.

Estimate Market Size: Use your research to estimate the size of your potential market. This will help you to determine if there is sufficient demand for your product or service to justify your investment.

Analyse Competition: Identify your direct and indirect competitors and analyse their strengths and weaknesses. This can help you to determine how you can differentiate your offering and compete in the market.

Conduct a SWOT Analysis: A SWOT analysis can help you to evaluate your strengths, weaknesses, opportunities, and threats. This can help you to identify potential challenges and develop a strategy to overcome them.

Evaluate Pricing and Profitability: Determine the price point at which you can offer your product or service while still maintaining profitability. This will help you to understand if your business is financially viable and if there is room in the market for your offering.

Test the Market: Before launching your product or service, test the market with a small-scale pilot project. This can help you to validate your assumptions, refine your offering, and identify potential challenges before investing heavily.

Evaluating market demand and competition is a critical step in determining the potential for success in a new business venture or expanding an existing one. By following these steps, you can identify opportunities in the market, develop a competitive strategy, and build a successful business.

Chapter 3

BUILD A STRONG ONLINE PRESENCE

Building a strong online presence is essential for businesses and individuals alike in today's digital age. A strong online presence can help you connect with your target audience, establish your brand, and grow your business.

Define your Target Audience: Before you start building your online presence, it's important to identify your target audience. Who are they? What are their interests? What problems do they need solving?

Create Valuable Content: Content is king when it comes to building a strong online presence.

Use Social Media: Social media is a powerful tool for building your online presence.

Engage with your Audience: Building a strong online presence is not just about creating content. It's also about engaging with your audience.

Monitor your Online Reputation: Your online reputation is important for building trust with your audience. Monitor your online reputation by setting up Google Alerts for your name or business, responding to reviews, and addressing any negative comments or feedback.

Building a strong online presence takes time and effort, but it's essential for success in today's digital age. By following these tips, you can establish your brand, connect with your target audience, and grow your business.

Developing a Website

Developing a website can be a daunting task, but if done right, it can be an incredibly rewarding experience. Here are some steps to help you develop a website:

Plan your Website: Before you start developing your website, it's important to plan it out. Determine what your website's purpose is, who your target audience is, and what content you want to include.

Choose a Domain Name and Hosting Provider: Your domain name is the address people will use to find your website, so choose a name that is easy to remember and relevant to your business or personal brand. You will also need to choose a hosting provider to store your website files and make your website accessible on the internet.

Design your Website: The design of your website is important for creating a positive user experience.

Develop your Website: This is where you will start building your website. You can use website builders like WordPress, Wix, or Squarespace to create your website, or you can hire a web developer to build a custom website for you.

Create Content: Your website's content is what will attract visitors and keep them coming back. Create high-quality content that is relevant to your target audience, and make sure it is optimised for search engines.

Test and Launch your Website: Before you launch your website, make sure to test it thoroughly to ensure it is functioning properly. Once you are satisfied with your website, launch it and promote it on social media and other marketing channels.

Maintain your Website: Your website is not a one-time project. It requires ongoing maintenance to ensure it is functioning properly and up to date. Regularly update your website's content, check for broken links, and make sure it is optimised for search engines.

Developing a website can be a complex process, but by following these steps, you can create a website that is functional, visually appealing, and optimised for search engines.

Creating Social Media Profiles

Creating social media profiles is an important step in building your online presence and connecting with your target audience. Here are some tips to help you create effective social media profiles:

Choose the Right Platforms: There are many social media platforms available, but not all of them are relevant to your business or personal brand.

Use Consistent Branding: Your social media profiles should reflect your brand.

Optimise your Profiles: Make sure your profiles are optimised for search engines by including relevant keywords in your bio and description. This will help your profiles appear in search results when people search for keywords related to your business or personal brand.

Create Engaging Content: Social media is all about engagement.

Promote your profiles: Once you have created your social media profiles, promote them on your website, email signature, and other marketing channels. This will help you attract more followers and grow your online presence.

Analyse your Performance: Use social media analytics tools to track your performance and see what content is resonating with your audience. Use this data to optimise your content and improve your social media strategy.

Creating social media profiles is an important step in building your online presence and connecting with your target audience. By following these tips, you can create effective social media profiles that reflect your brand and engage your audience.

Implementing SEO Strategies

Implementing effective SEO strategies is essential for businesses and website owners who want to attract more organic traffic and increase their online presence. Here are some comprehensive steps to implement SEO strategies:

Conduct a Website Audit: A website audit is the first step to identifying the areas that need improvement. The audit can help you determine which pages are performing well, which ones need improvement, and what technical issues need fixing. You can use a variety of tools such as Google Analytics, Google Search Console, and SEMrush to conduct an audit.

On-page Optimization: On-page optimization involves optimising the content on your website to make it more search engine friendly. This includes optimising page titles, meta descriptions, header tags, and alt tags.

Technical Optimization: Technical optimization involves improving the technical aspects of your website, such as website speed, mobile responsiveness, and website structure. Use tools such as Google PageSpeed Insights, GTmetrix, and Pingdom to analyse your website speed and make improvements.

Building Quality Backlinks is one of the most Important SEO Strategies: Quality backlinks can improve your website's authority and ranking in search engine results pages.

Create Quality Content: Creating quality content is essential for SEO success. Quality content can help attract more traffic to your website and improve your search engine rankings. Make sure your content is relevant, informative, and engaging.

Monitor and measure results: Monitoring and measuring the results of your SEO efforts is essential to identify areas that need improvement. Use tools such as Google Analytics and Google Search Console to monitor your website's performance and track your search engine rankings.

Implementing effective SEO strategies requires a combination of technical and creative skills. By conducting a website audit, conducting keyword research, optimising your website, building quality backlinks, creating quality content, and monitoring and measuring results, you can improve your website's visibility and ranking in search engine results pages.

Building an Email List

It allows businesses to engage with their target audience on a more personal level, establish trust and loyalty, and promote their products or services. Here are some comprehensive steps to building an email list:

Determine your Target Audience: Before building an email list, it's essential to know who you want to target. Determine your ideal customer persona and create a profile based on their demographics, interests, and behaviours.

Choose an Email Marketing Platform: There are various email marketing platforms available, such as Mailchimp, Constant Contact, AWeber, etc. Choose the one that best fits your business's needs and budget.

Create a Lead Magnet: A lead magnet is an incentive you offer to your audience in exchange for their email address. It can be a free ebook, webinar, template, or any valuable content that your target audience would find useful.

Create a Landing Page: A landing page is a dedicated web page designed to capture email addresses. It should include a clear headline, a brief description of the lead magnet, and a simple opt-in form that asks for the user's name and email address.

Promote your Lead Magnet: Promote your lead magnet through your website, blog, social media, and other marketing channels. Use paid advertising to increase its reach and exposure.

Optimise your Opt-in Forms: Ensure that your opt-in forms are easy to use and visually appealing. Use a clear and compelling call-to-action to encourage users to sign up.

Segment your Email List: Segmenting your email list allows you to personalise your email campaigns and send targeted messages to specific groups of subscribers based on their interests and behaviours.

Consistently provide value: Keep your subscribers engaged by consistently providing value through informative and relevant content. Avoid spamming their inboxes with sales pitches and promotional messages.

Monitor your Email Metrics: Regularly monitor your email metrics, such as open rates, click-through rates, and conversion rates. Use this data to optimise your email campaigns and improve your results.

Building an email list takes time and effort, but it's a valuable asset for any business. By following these steps, you can create a high-quality email list that engages your target audience and drives sales.

Creating Valuable Content

Creating valuable content is essential in today's digital landscape, where information is readily available to everyone.

The internet has made it easier for individuals and businesses to reach a vast audience, but it has also led to an abundance of content. Therefore, it is critical to create valuable content that resonates with your audience and sets you apart from the competition.

Tips for Creating Valuable Content:

Understand Your Audience: To create valuable content, you must first understand your target audience.

This includes their needs, interests, pain points, and goals. By understanding your audience, you can tailor your content to meet their needs and provide them with the information they are seeking.

Provide Unique Insights: To create valuable content, you need to provide unique insights that cannot be found elsewhere. This means conducting research, analysing data, and drawing conclusions that are not readily apparent.

By providing unique insights, you establish yourself as an expert in your field and provide value to your audience.

Solve Problems: People turn to the internet to find solutions to their problems. By creating content that addresses common issues or challenges your audience faces, you provide value to your audience. This can include how-to guides, step-by-step tutorials, and product reviews.

Be Authentic: In today's world, people crave authenticity. By being authentic in your content, you build trust with your audience. This means being honest about your experiences, sharing your personal story, and providing genuine recommendations.

Use Engaging Formats: Valuable content comes in various formats, including blog posts, videos, infographics, podcasts, and social media posts. By using engaging formats, you can capture your audience's attention and convey your message effectively.

Focus on Quality Over Quantity: Creating valuable content is not about churning out as much content as possible. It is about creating content that resonates with your audience and provides value.

Incorporate SEO: To ensure your valuable content reaches your target audience, you must incorporate search engine optimization (SEO) techniques.

This includes using relevant keywords, optimising your meta descriptions and titles, and using descriptive headers.

Creating valuable content requires a deep understanding of your audience, providing unique insights, solving problems, being authentic, using engaging formats, focusing on quality over quantity, and incorporating SEO.

By following these tips, you can create content that resonates with your audience, establishes your brand as an expert, and provides value.

Chapter 4

MONETIZE YOUR ONLINE BUSINESS

Monetising an online business involves generating revenue from the products or services offered on the website. There are various ways to monetize an online business, and the strategy that works best depends on the type of business and the target audience. Here are some ways to monetize an online business:

Advertising: One of the most popular ways to monetize an online business is through advertising. This involves displaying ads on your website and earning revenue based on the number of clicks or impressions generated.

To get started with advertising, you can sign up for ad networks like Google AdSense, which will provide you with ad codes to place on your website. You can also negotiate direct advertising deals with businesses and charge a flat fee for displaying their ads.

Affiliate Marketing: Affiliate marketing involves promoting other people's products on your website and earning a commission for every sale made through your unique affiliate link.

You can join affiliate programs of companies that are relevant to your niche and promote their products on your website through blog posts, reviews, or product comparisons.

Subscription-Based Models: If you offer premium content or services on your website, you can monetize your business through subscription-based models.

This involves charging a monthly or annual fee for access to exclusive content, tools, or services. Some examples of subscription-based models include online courses, membership sites, or premium content like podcasts or videos.

E-commerce: If you sell physical or digital products on your website, you can monetize your business through e-commerce. This involves setting up an online store and selling products directly to your customers. You can use platforms like Shopify or WooCommerce to create an online store, and you can also sell products on marketplaces like Amazon or Etsy.

Donations: If you offer valuable content or services for free, you can monetize your business through donations. This involves asking your audience to support your work through donations or contributions.

You can add a donation button to your website or use crowdfunding platforms like Patreon or Kickstarter to raise funds.

Selling Physical or Digital Products

Selling physical or digital products online can be a lucrative way to monetize an online business. However, there are several factors to consider when selling products online, including product selection, pricing, marketing, and fulfilment.

Here are some tips for selling physical or digital products online:

Selecting Products: Before you start selling products online, you need to decide what products to sell. You can sell physical products like clothing, electronics, or home goods, or digital products like e-books, courses, or software.

It's important to choose products that are in demand and align with your brand and target audience.

Pricing: Pricing is a critical factor in the success of any e-commerce business. Consider the cost of the product, shipping, and any other expenses you may incur, and factor in a margin for profit. You can also use pricing strategies like discounts or bundles to increase sales.

Marketing: Once you have selected your products and priced them appropriately, you need to market them effectively. You can use various marketing channels to promote your products, including social media, email marketing, paid advertising, and influencer marketing. It's important to create compelling product descriptions and images and to highlight the benefits of your products to your target audience.

Fulfilment: This involves managing the process of getting your products to your customers. For physical products, this typically involves storing inventory, packaging and shipping orders, and handling returns and exchanges.

You can handle fulfilment in-house or use a third-party logistics provider (3PL) to handle it for you. For digital products, fulfilment is typically automated, and customers receive a download link or access to an online course or software.

Payment Processing: To sell products online, you need to be able to accept payments from your customers. You can use a payment processor like PayPal, Stripe, or Square to securely process payments and manage transactions.

It's important to choose a payment processor that is easy to use and integrates with your e-commerce platform.

E-commerce Platform: To sell products online, you need an e-commerce platform that allows you to create an online store, manage inventory, process payments, and handle fulfilment.

It's important to choose an e-commerce platform that is easy to use and offers the features and integrations you need.

Offering Services

Offering services online can be a lucrative way to monetize an online business. Whether you offer consulting, coaching, design, writing, or other services, there are several factors to consider when offering services online, including pricing, marketing, and delivery. Here are some tips for offering services online:

Defining your Services: Before you start offering services online, you need to define what services you will offer.

Consider your skills, experience, and expertise, and choose services that align with your strengths and target audience. It's important to be clear about the scope of your services, the deliverables, and the timelines involved.

Pricing: Pricing is a critical factor in the success of any service-based business. You need to price your services competitively while still making a profit. Consider the value of your services, the market demand, and the competition, and factor in a margin for profit.

You can also use pricing strategies like packages or hourly rates to increase sales.

Marketing: Once you have defined your services and priced them appropriately, you need to market them effectively. You can use various marketing channels to promote your services, including social media, email marketing, content marketing, and networking.

It's important to create compelling service descriptions and case studies and to highlight the benefits of your services to your target audience.

Delivery: Delivery involves managing the process of providing your services to your clients. This includes communication, project management, and delivering the final product or service. You can use tools like project management software, video conferencing software, and collaboration tools to manage the delivery process.

It's important to communicate clearly with your clients and to manage their expectations throughout the process.

Payment Processing: To offer services online, you need to be able to accept payments from your clients. You can use a payment processor like PayPal, Stripe, or Square to securely process payments and manage transactions.

It's important to choose a payment processor that is easy to use and integrates with your invoicing and project management tools.

Service Agreement: To protect yourself and your clients, it's important to have a written service agreement that outlines the scope of your services, the deliverables, the timelines, and the payment terms.

You can use a template or hire a lawyer to draft a service agreement that meets your specific needs.

Offering services online can be a profitable way to monetize an online business. By defining your services, pricing them appropriately, marketing them effectively, and delivering them efficiently, you can build a successful service-based business online.

Creating and Selling Online Courses

Creating and selling online courses has become a popular way for individuals and businesses to share their knowledge and expertise with a global audience.

Online courses offer a flexible and convenient way for learners to acquire new skills and knowledge from the comfort of their own homes.

Choose a Topic and Define your Target Audience

The first step in creating an online course is to choose a topic that you are knowledgeable and passionate about. It is important to select a topic that has a target audience and is in demand. Once you have chosen your topic, define your target audience.

Who are they? What are their needs and interests? What are their pain points? Understanding your target audience will help you create a course that meets their needs and provides value.

Plan Your Course Content

Once you have chosen your topic and defined your target audience, it's time to plan your course content. Start by creating an outline of the topics you want to cover in your course.

Break down each topic into smaller sections and determine the order in which you will present them. Consider using multimedia content such as videos, images, and audio to make your course more engaging and interactive.

Create Your Course Content

With your course content planned out, it's time to create your course materials. Depending on your topic and teaching style, you may choose to create videos, written content, quizzes, assignments, or a combination of these.

Ensure that your course content is clear, concise, and easy to understand. Use examples and case studies to illustrate your points and make your course more relatable.

Choose a Learning Management System (LMS)

A learning management system (LMS) is a software application that allows you to create, manage, and deliver your online course. There are many LMS options available, including Teachable, Thinkific.

When choosing an LMS, consider the features you need, such as course hosting, payment processing, and student management.

Market Your Course

Once you have created your course and chosen an LMS, it's time to market your course. Start by creating a landing page that describes your course and its benefits.

Launch Your Course

With your course created and marketed, it's time to create and sell online courses. It has become a popular way for individuals and businesses to share their knowledge and expertise with a global audience.

Online courses offer a flexible and convenient way for learners to acquire new skills and knowledge from the comfort of their own homes.

Choosing an LMS is a critical step in creating and launching an online course. Your LMS will host your course content, manage payments and student data, and provide features that will make it easy for you to create and deliver a great learning experience.

There are many different options available, so take the time to research which one will best fit your needs. Once you've chosen an LMS, follow the steps below to get started with marketing and launching your course.

Creating a landing page is the first step to promoting your online course. This page should include information about what learners can expect from the course as well as how they can sign up.

Be sure to include social media buttons so that visitors can share the page with their networks. Email marketing is another great way to reach potential students - send out announcements about your newcourse using an email service like Mailchimp or Constant Contact.

And don't forget about paid advertising! Platforms like Google Adwords or Facebook Ads can help you reach even more people who might be interested in taking your class.

Now that you've got the basics down, it's time to start promoting your online course! Follow the tips above to get started reaching potential students and selling more courses.

Affiliate Marketing

This type of marketing is commonly used in e-commerce and online businesses, but can be used in other industries as well.

In affiliate marketing, the affiliate promotes the product or service of the business through various channels such as social media, blog posts, email marketing, or advertising.

When a customer clicks on the affiliate's unique tracking link and makes a purchase or performs a desired action, such as filling out a form or signing up for a newsletter, the affiliate receives a commission or a percentage of the sale.

Affiliate marketing is beneficial for both businesses and affiliates. Businesses can expand their reach by tapping into the network of affiliates who have access to a large audience.

This can help businesses reach new customers and increase sales. Affiliates, on the other hand, can earn a passive income by promoting products or services they believe in to their audience.

There are several types of affiliate marketing:

Pay-per-click (PPC) – In this model, affiliates are paid for each click they generate on the business's website. This model is less common than others, as businesses are less interested in paying for clicks that do not convert into sales.

Pay-per-lead (PPL) – In this model, affiliates are paid for each lead they generate for the business. A lead can be a sign-up form, a survey response, or any other action that shows interest in the business's product or service.

Pay-per-sale (PPS) – In this model, affiliates are paid for each sale they generate for the business. This is the most common type of affiliate marketing, as businesses are only paying for results.

Affiliate marketing can be a profitable source of income for affiliates who have a large and engaged audience.

To succeed in affiliate marketing, it's essential to choose the right products or services to promote and to create content that resonates with the audience. Additionally, building trust with the audience is crucial, as they are more likely to purchase a product or service recommended by someone they trust.

Affiliate marketing is an effective way for businesses to expand their reach and for affiliates to earn a passive income. With the right strategy and approach, affiliate marketing can be a win-win for both parties involved.

Advertising

Advertising is a marketing communication strategy that involves promoting products, services, or ideas to a target audience through various media channels such as print, television, radio, billboards, and online platforms.
The primary goal of advertising is to influence the audience's behaviour by raising awareness, generating interest, and driving action.

Advertising can be broadly categorised into two types: traditional and digital.
Traditional Advertising
Traditional advertising includes print, television, radio, outdoor, and direct mail. This

type of advertising is typically more expensive and has a broader reach.

Traditional advertising requires careful planning and execution to ensure maximum impact and ROI. It is also difficult to track the effectiveness of traditional advertising.

Digital Advertising

Digital advertising includes online, mobile, and social media advertising. This type of advertising is more cost-effective, has a more targeted reach, and provides greater transparency in terms of results tracking.

Digital advertising also allows for more interactive and engaging campaigns, as well as personalised messaging.

Types of Digital Advertising

Search Engine: Advertising Advertising through search engines such as Google, where businesses bid on keywords related to their products or services.

Social Media Advertising: Advertising through social media platforms such as Facebook, Twitter, and Instagram, where businesses can target specific demographics and interests.

Display Advertising: Advertising through banner ads on websites, where businesses can target specific websites or demographics.

Video Advertising: Advertising through video ads on platforms such as YouTube, where businesses can target specific demographics.

Native Advertising: Advertising that blends in with the platform's content, such as sponsored posts on social media.
Advertising is an essential aspect of marketing, as it helps businesses reach their target audience and achieve their goals.

Chapter 5

UTILISE MARKETING STRATEGIES

Marketing strategies are essential for businesses of all sizes to attract, engage, and retain customers.

These strategies include a range of techniques and approaches to promote products, services, and brands to target audiences. Utilising effective marketing strategies can help businesses increase their customer base, enhance brand awareness, and ultimately drive sales.

Here are some comprehensive steps to effectively utilise marketing strategies:

Identify your Target Audience: The first step in utilising marketing strategies is to identify your target audience.

Define your Marketing Goals: Set clear marketing goals that align with your business objectives. Examples of marketing goals include increasing website traffic, generating leads, improving brand recognition, or boosting sales.

Choose your Marketing Channels: There are numerous marketing channels available, including social media, email marketing, content marketing, search engine optimization (SEO), pay-per-click (PPC) advertising, and more.

Create Compelling Content: Develop high-quality content that is relevant, informative, and engaging. Use your content to educate, entertain, and inspire your target audience while promoting your products or services.

Implement a Lead Generation Strategy: Use lead generation tactics such as gated content, email opt-ins, or social media campaigns to capture contact information from potential customers. This will enable you to nurture leads through targeted email marketing campaigns or other personalised communication.

Measure your Results: Utilise analytics tools to measure the effectiveness of your marketing strategies. Analyse metrics such as website traffic, click-through rates, conversion rates, and social media engagement to evaluate the success of your campaigns.

Use this data to refine your marketing strategies and improve future performance.

Continuously Iterate: Marketing is an ongoing process, and it's essential to continuously iterate and improve your strategies.

Stay up-to-date with the latest marketing trends and technologies, and be willing to adapt your approach as needed to achieve your business goals.
Effectively utilising marketing strategies requires a comprehensive approach that incorporates audience targeting, goal-setting, channel selection, content creation,

Paid Advertising

Paid advertising, also known as pay-per-click (PPC) advertising, is a form of digital marketing where businesses pay to display their ads on search engines or social media platforms.

The primary benefit of paid advertising is that it can drive highly targeted traffic to a website or landing page. It allows businesses to reach a specific audience, based on demographics, interests, and behaviours, which can help increase the chances of conversions and sales.

There are various types of paid advertising, including search advertising, display advertising, social media advertising, and video advertising.

Search Advertising: This type of advertising involves displaying text ads on search engine results pages (SERPs) when users search for specific keywords. The ads are displayed at the top and bottom of the search results and are marked as "sponsored" or "ad." Google Ads and Microsoft Advertising are the most popular search advertising platforms.

Display Advertising: Display ads are visual ads, such as banners or images, that appear on websites or mobile apps. They are typically used for brand awareness campaigns and can be targeted based on user interests or behaviours.

Google Display Network, Facebook Audience Network, and programmatic advertising platforms are popular options for display advertising.

Social Media Advertising: This type of advertising involves displaying ads on social media platforms, such as Facebook, Instagram, Twitter, and LinkedIn. Social media ads can be targeted based on demographics, interests, behaviours, and even specific locations. They can also include various formats, such as images, videos, and carousels.

Video Advertising: Video ads are short video clips that are displayed on websites or social media platforms. They are used to drive brand awareness and engagement, and can be targeted based on user interests and behaviours.

YouTube, Facebook, and Instagram are popular platforms for video advertising.

When creating a paid advertising campaign, businesses must define their target audience, select the appropriate advertising platform, and set a budget for the campaign. They must also create compelling ad copy, choose relevant keywords, and select the appropriate targeting options.

Paid advertising can be expensive, and businesses must carefully monitor their campaigns to ensure they are getting a positive return on investment (ROI). They should track key metrics such as click-through rate (CTR), conversion rate, and cost per acquisition (CPA), and adjust their campaigns accordingly.

Paid advertising is a powerful tool for driving targeted traffic to a website or landing page. It can be an effective way to reach a specific audience and drive conversions and sales, but businesses must carefully monitor their campaigns to ensure they are getting a positive ROI.

Content Marketing

Content marketing is all about creating and sharing content that is informative, educational, and valuable to the target audience, with the goal of building trust, establishing credibility, and ultimately driving sales.

Content marketing involves the creation of various types of content, such as blog posts, articles, videos, social media posts, infographics, podcasts, and more. The content is designed to appeal to the target audience's interests and needs, rather than explicitly promoting a product or service.

The primary goal of content marketing is to attract and engage a specific target audience, rather than a mass audience. The content is designed to be informative, educational, and helpful, rather than simply promotional. By creating valuable content that is relevant and useful to the target audience, content marketing helps to build trust and establish credibility with potential customers.

There are several benefits to using content marketing as a marketing strategy, including:

Increased Brand Awareness: Content marketing can help to increase brand awareness by providing valuable and informative content that is shared across various platforms and channels.

Improved Search Engine Rankings: Creating high-quality content can help to improve a website's search engine rankings, making it easier for potential customers to find the company's website.

Increased Engagement: By providing valuable content that is relevant to the target audience, content marketing can help to increase engagement with potential customers.

Increased Conversions: Content marketing can help to drive conversions by building trust and establishing credibility with potential customers.

To create an effective content marketing strategy, it is important to identify the target audience, determine the types of content that will be most valuable to them, and create a plan for creating and sharing that content across various platforms and channels.

Overall, content marketing is a powerful marketing strategy that can help businesses to build trust, establish credibility, and ultimately drive profitable customer action.

By creating valuable content that is relevant and useful to the target audience, businesses can attract and engage potential customers, build relationships, and ultimately drive sales.

Influencer Marketing

Influencer Marketing is a marketing strategy that leverages the popularity and influence of individuals who have a large following on social media platforms to promote a brand's products or services. These individuals, known as influencers, have developed a loyal fanbase due to their engaging content, unique perspectives, and authentic voice.

Influencer marketing has gained immense popularity in recent years due to the increasing number of social media users and the decline in the effectiveness of traditional advertising methods.

By partnering with influencers, brands can tap into their followers' trust and loyalty and create a more meaningful and authentic connection with their target audience.

Types of Influencer Marketing

There are several types of influencer marketing campaigns that brands can use to engage with their target audience. These include:

Sponsored Content: This is the most common type of influencer marketing, where a brand pays an influencer to create and post content about their products or services on their social media accounts.

Affiliate Marketing: In this type of influencer marketing, influencers receive a commission on every sale made through their unique referral link.

Brand Ambassadorship: This involves a long-term partnership between a brand and an influencer, where the influencer becomes a brand ambassador and promotes the brand's products or services on an ongoing basis.

Product Placement: This involves a brand sending products to influencers for them to use or feature in their content.

Choosing the Right Influencer

Brands should look for influencers whose values align with their brand and whose followers match their target audience. They should also consider the influencer's engagement rate, authenticity, and reputation.

Measuring the Success of Influencer Marketing

Brands can measure the success of their influencer marketing campaigns by tracking metrics such as engagement rate, reach, impressions, website traffic, and sales. They can also use tools such as Google Analytics, social media analytics, and influencer marketing platforms to track and analyse their results.

Benefits of Influencer Marketing

Influencer marketing offers several benefits to brands, including:

Increased Brand Awareness: Influencers have a large following on social media, which can help brands increase their brand awareness and reach a wider audience.

Authenticity: Influencers are seen as trusted sources of information, and their endorsement of a brand's products or services can create a more authentic connection with their followers.

Higher Engagement: Influencer marketing can lead to higher engagement rates than traditional advertising methods, as influencers have a more personal connection with their followers.

Cost-Effective: Influencer marketing can be cost-effective, as brands can choose influencers with a smaller following

Social Media Marketing

Social media marketing is the practice of using social media platforms to promote a brand, product, or service. It involves creating and sharing content on social media networks in order to engage with a target audience and build brand awareness, ultimately leading to increased website traffic and conversions.

The rise of social media has revolutionised the way businesses connect with their customers. Social media platforms such as Facebook, Twitter, Instagram, LinkedIn, and Pinterest offer businesses a way to reach a vast audience at a relatively low cost.

Benefits of Social Media Marketing:

Increased brand awareness: Social media platforms provide a large audience for businesses to promote their brand and reach potential customers.

Improved Customer Engagement: Social media provides a direct channel for businesses to communicate with their customers and receive feedback.

Increased Website Traffic: Social media can drive traffic to a business's website through links shared in posts.

Cost-effective: Social media marketing is often less expensive than traditional advertising methods.

Improved Customer Loyalty: Regular engagement with customers through social media can help build brand loyalty.

Social Media Marketing Strategy:

Set Goals: Define what you want to achieve with your social media marketing efforts. Whether it's brand awareness, lead generation, or customer engagement, having clear goals will help guide your strategy.

Know your Audience: Identify your target audience and tailor your content and messaging to their interests and needs.

Choose the Right Platforms: Determine which social media platforms are best suited for your business and target audience.

Create Engaging Content: Develop a content strategy that includes a mix of text, images, and videos that resonates with your audience.

Engage with your Audience: Respond to comments and messages, and actively participate in conversations related to your industry or niche.

Analyse your Results: Use social media analytics tools to measure the success of your efforts and make adjustments to your strategy as needed.

By following these steps and continually analysing and adapting your strategy, you can create a successful social media marketing campaign.

Search Engine Marketing (SME)

It encompasses a wide range of tactics that are designed to drive traffic to a website by increasing its visibility and relevance to search engine users.

SEM involves both paid and organic methods to drive traffic to a website. Paid search advertising, also known as pay-per-click (PPC) advertising, involves bidding on relevant keywords to display ads at the top or bottom of the SERPs.

These ads are typically marked as sponsored and are shown to users who enter a query that matches the advertiser's keyword bids. Advertisers pay only when someone clicks on their ad, which makes this a cost-effective method of advertising.

Organic search engine optimization, on the other hand, involves optimising a website's content and structure to improve its relevance and authority for specific keywords. This includes optimising website content, improving website structure and navigation, and building high-quality backlinks from other authoritative websites. These efforts can take time to see results, but they can be a cost-effective way to increase traffic to a website in the long term.

Both paid and organic methods can be used together to create a comprehensive SEM strategy. This can include identifying the most relevant keywords and creating content that targets those keywords, as well as bidding on those keywords for paid search advertising.

By combining these tactics, businesses can maximise their online visibility and drive targeted traffic to their websites.

SEM offers Several Advantages to Businesses, Including:

Increased Visibility: SEM helps businesses increase their visibility and reach a larger audience by appearing at the top of the SERPs for relevant keywords.

Targeted Traffic: By bidding on relevant keywords and optimising website content for those keywords, businesses can drive targeted traffic to their websites and increase the likelihood of converting those visitors into customers.

Cost-effective Advertising: PPC advertising allows businesses to pay only for clicks on their ads, making it a cost-effective way to advertise online.

Measurable Results: SEM allows businesses to track their advertising and website performance, providing valuable insights into what is working and what is not.

Chapter 6

UTILISING ANALYTICS FOR BUSINESS SUCCESS.

Utilising analytics involves using these insights to improve business performance and achieve strategic goals. In today's data-driven world, utilising analytics has become a crucial part of any organisation's success.

There are several types of analytics that organisations can use, including descriptive, diagnostic, predictive, and prescriptive analytics. Descriptive analytics provides insights into what has happened in the past, while diagnostic analytics helps identify the root cause of a problem.

Predictive analytics uses historical data to forecast future trends, and prescriptive analytics offers recommendations on the best course of action to take.

Utilising Analytics can Benefit an Organisation in Several Ways, Including:

Improving Operational Efficiency: Analytics can help identify inefficiencies and bottlenecks in a process, enabling organisations to streamline operations and improve productivity.

Enhancing Customer Experience: Analytics can help organisations understand customer behaviour and preferences, allowing them to deliver personalised experiences that meet their customers' needs.

Reducing Costs: Analytics can help organisations identify cost-saving opportunities by optimising resource allocation, reducing waste, and minimising operational expenses.

Increasing Revenue: Analytics can help organisations identify new revenue streams and opportunities, enabling them to capitalise on emerging trends and market demands.

To utilise analytics effectively, organisations need to have the right tools and resources in place. This includes investing in data management systems, hiring skilled data analysts, and providing training to employees on how to interpret and use data effectively.

Utilising analytics is essential for organisations looking to stay competitive in today's data-driven marketplace.

By leveraging data insights, organisations can improve operational efficiency, enhance customer experiences, reduce costs, and increase revenue, ultimately leading to greater business success.

Setting up Google Analytics

Google Analytics is a powerful tool that helps website owners track and analyse website traffic, user behaviour, and engagement.

Setting up Google Analytics is essential for any website owner who wants to understand their website's performance, improve user experience, and optimise their marketing strategies. Here's a comprehensive guide on how to set up Google Analytics:

Sign Up for Google Analytics

To start setting up Google Analytics, you need to sign up for an account. And You will then be prompted to sign in to your Google account or create one if you don't have one.

Set Up Your Property

Once you have signed in to your Google account, you will be taken to the Google Analytics setup page. You will need to provide some basic information about your website, including your website name, URL, industry, and time zone. Google Analytics will then create a "property" for your website, which is a unique tracking ID that you will need to add to your website.

Install the Tracking Code

After setting up your property, you will be given a tracking code that you need to add to your website. The tracking code is a small snippet of JavaScript code that tracks visitor data and sends it to Google Analytics.

You can either add the tracking code manually to each page of your website, or you can use a website builder or content management system (CMS) that integrates with Google Analytics.

If you're adding the tracking code manually, copy the tracking code provided by Google Analytics and paste it into the header section of your website.

Verify Tracking Code Installation

After adding the tracking code to your website, you should verify that it is working correctly. To do this, go back to the Google Analytics website and click the "Admin" button in the bottom left corner of the page.

Google Analytics will show you if your tracking code is installed correctly and how many visitors it has tracked.

Set Up Goals and Funnels

Goals and funnels are important metrics that help you track and measure the effectiveness of your website.

Goals are specific actions that you want visitors to take on your website, such as making a purchase or filling out a contact form. Funnels are the steps that visitors take to complete a goal, such as adding a product to their cart and completing the checkout process.

To set up goals and funnels, go to the "Admin" section of Google Analytics and select "Goals". From there, you can create a new goal and define the steps that visitors need to take to complete it.

Analyse Your Data

Once you have set up Google Analytics and added your tracking code to your website, you can start analysing your data. Google Analytics provides a wide range of reports and metrics that can help you understand your website.

Analysing Website Traffic and User Behaviour

Analysing website traffic and user behaviour is an essential aspect of digital marketing. It involves collecting, analysing, and interpreting data related to website visitors and their behaviour to gain insights and make data-driven decisions.

By understanding website traffic and user behaviour, businesses can optimise their website, content, and marketing strategies to improve user engagement, increase conversions, and boost ROI.

There are several tools and techniques used to analyse website traffic and user behaviour. Some of the popular ones are:

Web Analytics: Web analytics tools like Google Analytics and Adobe Analytics provide businesses with comprehensive data related to website traffic, user behaviour, and conversion rates.

They offer insights into user demographics, traffic sources, time spent on site, page views, bounce rates, and conversion rates. This information can be used to identify areas of improvement and optimise website performance.

User Surveys: User surveys provide businesses with direct feedback from website visitors. They can help identify pain points, areas of improvement, and what users like or dislike about a website. User surveys can be used to improve website content, user experience, and conversion rates.

A/B Testing: A/B testing involves testing two versions of a website or landing page to see which one performs better. By comparing the performance of the two versions, businesses can identify which design elements, copy, or calls to action resonate better with their target audience.

Analysing website traffic and user behaviour can help businesses in several ways, including:

Improving User Experience: By understanding user behaviour, businesses can identify areas of improvement and optimise their website and content to provide a better user experience. This can lead to increased user engagement, higher conversion rates, and improved customer satisfaction.

Boosting SEO: By analysing website traffic, businesses can identify which keywords and search terms are driving traffic to their site. This information can be used to optimise website content and improve SEO rankings.

Increasing Conversions: By analysing user behaviour, businesses can identify which pages or elements of a website are leading to conversions. This information can be used to optimise website content and design to increase conversion rates.

Improving Marketing Strategies: By analysing website traffic and user behaviour, businesses can identify which marketing channels are driving the most traffic and conversions. This information can be used to optimise marketing strategies and allocate resources more effectively.

Analysing website traffic and user behaviour is an essential aspect of digital marketing. By collecting and analysing data related to website visitors and their behaviour, businesses can gain insights and make data-driven decisions to optimise their website, content, and marketing strategies.

Making Data-Driven Decisions

Making data-driven decisions is a process of using available data and analytics to inform business decisions, strategies, and actions. Data-driven decision-making relies on the collection, analysis, and interpretation of relevant data to identify patterns, trends, and insights.

This information is then used to make informed decisions, measure progress, and optimise performance.

Data-driven decision-making can be applied across all business functions, including marketing, sales, operations, finance, and customer service. The goal is to use data to improve business outcomes, increase efficiency, and drive growth.

There are several steps involved in making data-driven decisions:

Define the Problem: The first step in making data-driven decisions is to clearly define the problem or opportunity. This involves understanding the business objective, identifying the key metrics to measure success, and determining the data needed to inform the decision.

Collect Relevant Data: Once the problem is defined, the next step is to collect relevant data. This involves gathering data from various sources, such as customer surveys, website analytics, social media platforms, and CRM systems.

Analyse the Data: The collected data is then analysed to identify patterns, trends, and insights. This involves using statistical methods, such as regression analysis, correlation analysis, and time-series analysis, to identify relationships and patterns in the data.

Interpret the Results: After analysing the data, the next step is to interpret the results. This involves drawing conclusions and making informed decisions based on the insights gained from the analysis.

Take Action: The final step is to take action based on the insights gained from the data analysis. This may involve implementing changes to business strategies, optimising processes, or launching new marketing campaigns.

Making data-driven decisions can offer several benefits for businesses, including:
Improved Performance: By using data to inform decisions, businesses can optimise performance, increase efficiency, and drive growth.

Reduced Risk: Data-driven decision-making can help reduce the risk of making poor decisions based on assumptions or guesswork.

Better Customer Experience: By using data to understand customer behaviour and preferences, businesses can improve the customer experience and increase customer satisfaction.

Increased ROI: By using data to optimise marketing and sales strategies, businesses can increase ROI and achieve higher revenue growth.

Making data-driven decisions is an essential aspect of modern business. By using data to inform decisions, businesses can optimise performance, reduce risk, improve the customer experience, and achieve higher revenue growth. The process involves defining the problem, collecting relevant data, analysing the data, interpreting the results, and taking action based on the insights gained from the analysis.

Conclusion

In conclusion, building wealth through online business can be a rewarding and fulfilling journey, but it requires a strategic and disciplined approach.

The key to success is identifying a viable business opportunity, developing a solid plan, executing it with precision, and continuously adapting to market changes.

It's essential to have a clear understanding of your target audience and their needs, as well as the competitive landscape. You should also have a well-defined value proposition that sets you apart from others in your niche.

Once you have a viable business idea, you'll need to create a detailed plan that outlines your goals, strategies, and tactics for achieving them. This plan should include a budget, marketing strategy, sales strategy, and a timeline for achieving your objectives.

In addition to having a solid plan, it's crucial to stay disciplined and focused on your goals. This means avoiding distractions, staying motivated, and consistently taking action towards your objectives.

Another key to building wealth through online business is to leverage technology and automation wherever possible. This includes using tools and software to automate repetitive tasks, streamline workflows, and improve efficiency.

It's essential to stay up-to-date on industry trends and adapt your strategies accordingly. This requires ongoing learning and development, as well as a willingness to experiment and try new approaches.

Building wealth through online business requires a combination of strategic planning, disciplined execution, technological savvy, and continuous learning and adaptation.

With the right approach and mindset, however, it's possible to achieve financial freedom and create a successful and fulfilling online business.

Note................

www.ingramcontent.com/pod-product-compliance
Lightning Source LLC
Chambersburg PA
CBHW070920220526
45467CB00004B/1493